BMX RIDER
by Gary Poole

Modern Publishing
A Divison of Unisystems, Inc.
New York, New York 10022
Printed in Canada

Cover Design: Marker II Studio
Front Cover Photo: Focus on Sports
Back Cover Photo: Associated Press/Wide World Photo
Book Design: Judith Teener Graphic Design

Book Number: 10330
ISBN Number: 0-87449-019-7

TABLE OF CONTENTS

A high-flying BMXer in action! Steve Giberson BMX ACTION Magazine

INTRODUCTION

BMX! No, it's not a subway line in New York. It's one of the fastest growing sports in the nation and it's spreading worldwide. Why? Because young people love it! And their parents love it, too! That's a rare and winning combination in any sport. When you've got your parents behind you, you're on the right track. The BMX track!

An estimated 300,000 riders compete in hundreds of national and local BMX races in classes divided by age, sex and skill. The ages range from as low as six and under to as high as seventeen and over. Most of the riders are between the ages of ten and sixteen.

Officials of the sport assure parents that BMX racing is safer than football or soccer! No rider has ever been permanently disabled in a BMX racing accident.

Serious riders say practice makes perfect, just

as in any other sport. Some ride as much as twenty-five miles a day. Others lift weights to keep in shape. And they are constantly taking their bikes apart and putting them back together again hoping to improve their performance.

Besides competing, thousands of young folks ride BMX bikes just for fun. Wearing goggles, heavy nylon pants and helmets, the riders look like hockey players rather than bike riders. They're exciting to watch as they sail into the air and drop down for hairpin turns.

How did it all begin? Where did it start? What were the first BMX bikes? Did these strange little bikes just suddenly appear from out of nowhere? There are no quick answers to those questions! BMX came up the hard way from the streets and vacant lots, spinning its wheels through mud and dirt, grinding its way to the top until it finally took America by storm!

THE HISTORY OF BMX

Motorcycle racing is called. *motocross*. It is a race in which grown men ride lightweight motorcycles over rugged courses. The word motocross comes from *motorcycle* and *cross-country*. So out of this came bicycle motocross or BMX.

The exact beginnings of BMX racing are hard to pinpoint, but it's safe to say that it started happening around 1969 in California. It began as an imitation of motorcycle racing. The kids who attended motorcycle races in those days brought along their bikes. After the races, they simply hung around until everybody went home. Then they took off out onto the track and staged their own races on bicycles without motors.

Many of the kids rode bicycles called Sting-Rays which were made by the Schwinn Bicycle Company. The Sting-Rays seemed best suited at the time for dirt track racing. Of course, the young

Sidewalk stunts can be done anywhere. Steve Giberson FREESTYLIN' Magazine

people who were into this also hung around their local bicycle shop and began modifying their bikes. They stripped off the side stands, reflectors and chain guards to reduce excess weight. Some even managed to have crossbars welded to brace their handlebars. These specially modified handlebars are called *butterfly* bars.

On these modified bikes, young people began doing wheelies and jumps. Then they'd take off as fast as they could pedal along dirt trails through fields, forests and parks, anywhere there was room to move.

Jumping, wheelies and riding fast weren't enough, so dirt tracks began to spring up in vacant lots in the neighborhoods so kids could race. The tracks just sort of happened as the riders began to race wherever they could. Ever take a walk through a forest along a dirt path and wonder how that path got started? Through repeated use, that's how. And that's how the first tracks began.

Finally, an enterprising promoter invited riders to race on a track he'd built in a big vacant lot in Long Beach, California. Word spread and riders began showing up from neighboring towns. The track had everything a rider could want—jumps, turns, waterholes and banks. It was practically a duplicate of a motorcycle track. The riders found out about other races through word of mouth. If you went to a race, you heard about the next race, and so on. They were a tight little group, but they weren't to remain little for long!

BMX racing continued to gain in popularity and by 1973 races were being held all over Southern California. Then along came Ernie Alexander. A former motorcycle race promoter, he founded the National Bicycle Association (NBA) and began setting rules and regulations for BMX racing. He divided the riders into different age groups and came up with the Novice and Expert divisions and the three-moto eliminations. A *moto,* is a heat race.

Now that BMX racing was getting organized, it attracted the attention of some motorcycle manufacturers. Strangely, the large bicycle companies stayed out of it in the beginning. They took a wait-and-see stance. Some parts manufacturers began making specialized equipment so that riders could modify their existing bikes. For example, Goodyear came out with a knobby-tread tire. The bikes were still backyard, garage-made, do-it-yourself jobs, a frame from here, a wheel from there or a pedal from somewhere else.

With the big bicycle maufacturers staying out of the picture, some small custom frameset builders began making bikes specially for BMX racing. They were to become some of the famous names in BMX today—like Mongoose and Red Line.

While all this was happening, BMX didn't even have a name. It was sort of informally called "dirt bike racing." It wasn't until a monthly newspaper called Bicycle Motorcross News was published that the name BMX took hold. People began referring to that newspaper as the "BMX News," and the rest, they say, is history.

BMX spread to other states. Races began springing up in Arizona, Oklahoma, Georgia and Florida. Racers and their parents (who were now hooked) often traveled hundreds of miles just to be in a race. It wasn't for the prize money, either. In fact, in those days there was no prize money and everybody had to pay their own expenses. It wasn't until later that sponsors came into the picture and even then they only supplied the bikes and parts. There was no money involved.

Gradually, full sponsorships occurred and "factory riders" emerged. Bike makers and related companies began plowing money into the sport, sponsoring races and "factory teams." A factory team consists of several riders whose travel expenses are paid by the sponsor.

How do you get picked for a factory team? Sponsors say they pick riders for racing potential, looks and appeal on the market. After all, they are going to be representing their products. A rider has to be personable and have a good family background, and he or she must have a C-plus average in school.

In 1976, NBA's Alexander promoted a set of seven national races to determine a national champion. He was getting membership applications for track sanctions from all over the country, from California to New Jersey.

The NBA National series in 1976 brought even more attention to BMX racing. States had been conducting races and coming up with their own state champions. Finally, by entering every race in the series, Scot Breithaupt emerged with the Grand National Championship. It wasn't long before the next step occurred—Professional BMX Racing.

Professional BMX racing began in 1977. Having a pro league would certainly add respect and prestige to the new sport. A meeting was held with the top sixteen and over experts. More rules and regulations were made concerning age, eligibility and amateur status. BMX was becoming serious business!

At first, the purse for winning a pro race was small. Sometimes the winner would walk off with only $20 for his efforts. But that was okay with the riders. They had been collecting trophies all those years, so any amount of money, no matter how small, looked good to them. It was a beginning.

As crowds grew larger and the popularity of BMX racing continued to rise, the purses grew. Within two years a winning rider could take home as much as $1,000!

Competition between the ABA (American Bicycle Association) and the NBL (National Bicycle League) grew, and so did the winnings. In 1979, the ABA awarded their Number One Pro a van valued at $13,000!

Now, sponsorship of riders has become bigtime business. Stars are placed on a guaranteed salary with the added bonus of all expense paid travel. Then there's the money to be picked up from commercials and endorsements of products.

No questions about it. BMX is bigtime! It's come a long way from the vacant lots, the streets and the old dirt paths created by countless wheelies and jumps as riders blasted off as fast as they could pedal!

SAFETY

How safe is BMX bike racing? Since its humble vacant lot beginnings in 1969, BMX racing has proven itself to be among the safest sports for young people. The reason for this is, BMX people, track designers and race organizers put safety first. The tracks themselves are designed to reduce the possibility of accidents.

The government has issued standards and requirements for strength and durability in bicycles, and manufacturers produce bikes that exceed these standards.

The racing rules are strict. Each rider is required to wear a crash helmet, mouth guard, long pants and racing jerseys. It is required that certain parts of the BMX bike be padded (Rad Pads) to reduce the chance of injury.

If the sport is so safe, why all these precautions? The answer is simple. For years BMX racing had no

All geared up and ready to race! Steve Giberson BMX ACTION Magazine

14

strict rules and regulations, and EVEN THEN, the safety record ranked better than football or soccer.

More proof of the safety of BMX racing comes from the insurance companies themselves. Sanctioned BMX races must carry insurance, and while insurance rates for other sporting events continue to rise, rates for BMX races remain low. You can bet if the sport was considered dangerous, those insurance rates would go sky high.

The NBL and ABA work hard to keep that good safety record intact. They make sure that the tracks are designed to be exciting and challenging to the riders, but safety comes first in any track design.

Years ago, young people racing wore only jeans and perhaps, a leather jacket and an old hand-me-down motorcycle helmet. Now, all accessories are specially designed for BMX racing—from helmets, pants, shirts, shoes, elbow guards, right down to the gloves they wear to grip the handlebars. So when you watch a BMX race, the best thing is not to worry. Just relax and enjoy the excitement!

BMX riders making moto history! Steve Giberson BMX ACTION Magazine

GEAR AND EQUIPMENT

Looking for your first BMX bike can make you dizzy. There are over forty different brands to choose from. To add to the confusion, a lot of them are made by major bicycle companies like Schwinn, Ross and Raleigh. Then there are companies that are exclusively BMX, like: Kuwahara (used by the youngsters in the movie *E.T.*), Mongoose, Diamond Back, Hutch, Skyway, Jag, Rhino, Torker, Robinson, Patterson and others with initials like CW, JMC, SE and GT. No wonder a beginner's eyes glaze when asked to select a bike from this crowd!

What should you do when it comes time to pick your first bike? The best advice is not to spend a lot of money on it. You're a beginner, and you're going to need a bike to learn on.

It is important that your first bike be durable. It's going to take a beating from jumps and spills and spinouts while you are learning this new kind of riding called BMX. Therefore, your first bike should be just a little bit heavier than the all out racing machines. That's what BMX riders call their bikes—machines—even though they don't have motors.

Prices may vary in different parts of the country, but your starter bike should cost around $140 or $150 or so. BMX bikes can cost upwards to $500 and more! So be cautious. You or your parents don't want to spend that kind of money until you are ready.

A lot depends on what you plan to use your BMX bike for. If you want it just for fun, then your starter bike is all you'll need. If you're planning on getting into serious racing, then you'll eventually graduate on to the more lightweight, faster models.

When you are shopping for a BMX bike, you have a choice. You can buy one that is factory assembled or you can build one yourself from a frameset and components that you feel are right for you.

Most people start out buying a factory assembled bike. They are well-made and will do the job for you. However, you must be sure to get a bike that is set correctly for you, your weight and size.

There are great bicycle shops in every city and town in this country. Talk to other people and find out where the BMX crowd hangs out. Then visit that shop. More often than not, you'll find the dealer there more than ready to discuss your problems and recommend a bike that is correct for you.

A word of advice: Don't be too quick in making your decision. Go to as many bicycle shops as you can. Listen to what dealers and other riders have to say. Buying a bike is like buying a pair of shoes. It has

Whether you are racing or just freestylin', safety pads are a must.
Steve Giberson BMX ACTION Magazine

to fit, or else you're in for a lot of problems.

Some riders need smaller handlebars and lighter cranks. Others need larger handlebars and bigger cranks. Go to the local BMX races. You'll find the riders there willing to talk freely about the differences in bikes. In fact, it's about *all* they talk about!

There are BMX bikes for everybody: minis for the youngest riders, midis for the pre-teens, regular size for the average rider (between 12-16 years old) and larger bikes for the pros. You can't always go by age, either. If you're 12 years old and six feet tall, you don't want a bike that the average 12-year-old would ride.

Now, you say, "But BMX bikes are all 'little'

bikes!" Not true. Sure, they all have the same 20" diameter wheels, but the frameset and other components are designed for riders of different sizes. So you can see a guy who's over six feet tall comfortably riding what looks like a little BMX bike! He's simply found the correct components to fit his size. Again, it's like buying shoes.

If you want to race, you'll need a freewheel bike with alloy wheels. A freewheel bike has hand-operated brakes so it's easier to control. Less expensive bikes have foot-operated coaster brakes which are great fun for riding and freestyle tricks, but not good for racing.

How do you know if a bike is right for you? It has to feel right. And only you can tell that. It has to be comfortable. The bars shouldn't cramp your wrists. You should be able to reach them from the sitting position with your back straight. The seat should be adjusted so you can pedal comfortably while sitting. The handlebars and the seat should be in the correct position that's comfortable for you. This is important whether you're riding just for fun or for serious racing (which is also fun, make no mistake about that).

Another thing to remember is that a properly set up bike is *safer*, whether you're racing or simply riding around town. You're more in control, and when you're in control of your machine, you are a safe rider.

Suppose you have an old bike that you want to customize into a BMX bike? The same rules apply. Get the components that are right for you and set the bike up properly.

Most riders make mistakes with the handlebar

adjustments. They sometimes tilt the bars too far forward. Moving the bars too far forward makes the bike hard to control. If you feel you need more room for your legs, it may not be the handlebars that need adjusting. It could be that you are using the wrong size frame. If your bike is not set up properly, you'll know about it soon enough with sore wrists and backaches.

One of the best ways to find out if a bike is right for you is to try out various friends' bikes. See how they feel to you. Try and pick those friends who are about your size and weight. When you find a bike that feels right for you, you'll be more knowledge-able when you talk with a dealer. It always helps if a dealer feels you know what you're talking about.

PARTS OF THE BIKE

GRIPS

You'll need good grips on your handlebars. Try to avoid odd-shaped grips. They may look flashy, but you might find only one position on them that is comfortable for your hands. A rubber grip with a round shape that has a good tread pattern and soft rubber is the best. Hard plastic grips tend to give you blisters and they are more apt to slip off. Another good tip—always wear gloves when you ride to race. You'll need them, and you'll be glad you did.

SAFETY OR RAD PADS

Even if you don't race, you should have a set of safety pads (rad pads) on your bike. They are required at races, and you'll be glad they are there if you accidentally hit your knee or face against the

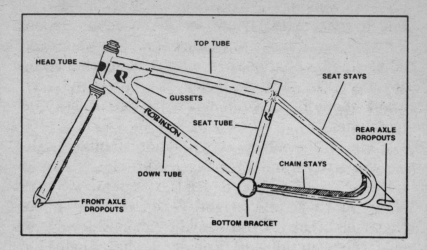

HEAD TUBE

TOP TUBE

GUSSETS

SEAT STAYS

SEAT TUBE

REAR AXLE DROPOUTS

ROBINSON

DOWN TUBE

CHAIN STAYS

FRONT AXLE DROPOUTS

BOTTOM BRACKET

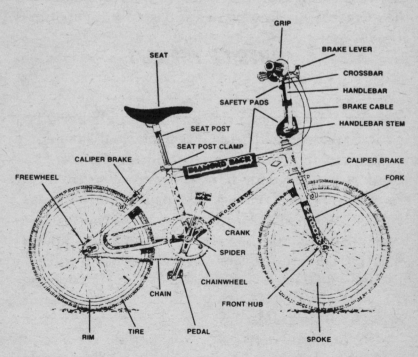

GRIP

BRAKE LEVER

SEAT

CROSSBAR

HANDLEBAR

SAFETY PADS

BRAKE CABLE

HANDLEBAR STEM

SEAT POST

CALIPER BRAKE

SEAT POST CLAMP

CALIPER BRAKE

FREEWHEEL

DIAMOND BACK

FORK

CRANK

SPIDER

CHAINWHEEL

CHAIN

FRONT HUB

RIM

TIRE

PEDAL

SPOKE

BMX ACTION Wizard Publications, Inc.

stem or crossbar. They give vital protection.

HANDLEBARS AND STEMS ────────────

Handlebars are the control center of your bike. They are simply a piece of tubing shaped for comfortable gripping and control. A tubular crossbar braces them against bending and are straight, although some may be V-shaped. A stem is simply a mount for the handlebar. It clamps the handlebar so you can adjust it into the correct position.

FRAMES AND FORKS ─────────────

The frame and fork are the heart of the BMX bike. Together they are called the frameset. The best are built from strong, light steels called chrome-moly and chrome-alloy. The frameset is the core of the bike. From this all other components are added.

TIRES ──────────────────

There are different tire tread patterns depending on the type of riding you plan to do. At first glance all tires may look alike, but upon closer examination, you'll see the differences. Large knobby treads increase traction in heavy mud or loose sand. Others are tight close-packed treads which are best for street use and hard-packed surfaces. In addition to black, tires come in colors like red, yellow and blue to go with or contrast with your frame.

SADDLE ─────────────────

The shotgun saddle is best used for racing. Its seat is aerodynamically designed so that it looks as though it were shot full of holes. Hence, the name, shotgun. The seat is hard, not soft. There's not much time for sitting down during a BMX race. Most riders raise their seat high to stabilize the bike in tight corners.

CRANKS

The strongest and least expensive cranks are the one-piece constructed all-steel cranks. These are used on most BMX bikes. Cranks come in various lengths depending on the size of the bike and the rider. There is also a three-piece aluminum-arm crankset on some BMX bikes. Its light weight appeals to younger riders who aren't very big in weight or size.

FREEWHEELS

Freewheels only propel the bike forward. If you try to backpedal and brake, it won't happen. Therefore on a Freewheel bike you'll need Caliper brakes. They are the same type as found on regular 10-speed bikes and are mounted on the handlebars. A small lever on the handlebar activates the brake. Freewheel bikes are used in racing.

COASTER BRAKES

Coaster brakes are used on freestyle-type bikes and others that are made for BMX riding, but not for racing. You simply reverse the pedal and brake.

PEDALS

Pedals come in two styles, rat trap and platform. Rat trap pedals get their name because the outer metal edge has a jagged cut that looks like teeth on some sort of animal trap. Those teeth grip the foot and keep it form slipping. The platform pedals are shaped and designed for traction and small studs provide a non-slip footsure surface.

WHEELS

There are two kinds of wheels: mag and spoke. Mag wheels are one-piece molded plastic and have built-in hubs. They're tough and can take a lot of rough treatment if you're into trick riding. However, they are too heavy for serious racing. The most commonly used are the spoke wheels. Aluminum rims (called alloys) come in various sizes and are the number one choice among riders.

HUBS

Sealed bearing or precision hubs keep the dirt out and stay roller smooth longer. There's less maintenance on these than unsealed hubs. Most pros, however, prefer the precision loose-ball type hubs.

NUMBER PLATE

If you are a racer, a number plate is required. Even if you're not racing, a number plate just makes a bike look better and they come in all designs and colors.

Working on your bike, keeping it clean, running smooth and at its top performance is fun. You'll be amazed at what you can do with what you have. All you need is BMX fever.

Don't let it bother you if your bike isn't the fanciest bike in town or in your neighborhood. The important thing is to learn how to ride it and become good at it. Your starter bike is your pal. It doesn't have to be top-notch for you to have fun and it will teach you a lot. Besides after a few races, your whole attitude on bikes will change and you'll have better ideas about what kind of racing bike is right for you.

————————— SUMMARY OF TIPS —————————

1. Talk to riders. Learn all you can from them about BMX bikes.

2. Visit various dealers. Tell them your needs. Listen. But don't buy right away. Take your time!

3. Don't spend much money on your first BMX bike. Your starter bike shouldn't cost more than $140-$150. Prices may vary with the economy, but that's around the current price range.

4. Test ride some of your friends' bikes to help find out which one feels right for you. Always test ride any bike you're buying!

5. Be sure your bike is a freewheel if you plan to race. Foot operated coaster bikes are for other types of BMX riding.

6. When you buy your bike make sure the handlebars and seat are positioned correctly for you. Ask the store dealer or some other expert to help you.

WHAT TO WEAR?

HELMETS

Racing is not the only way to enjoy your BMX bike. Many people own BMX bikes for the pleasure of riding them or jumping and doing stunt-type tricks. For whatever purpose you have a BMX bike, you should wear a good helmet if you're going to try jumping or doing tricks.

Buying a helmet is just like buying a BMX bike. You have to get one that's right for you in size and comfort. There are a couple of types to consider. There's the full-face helmet. It will give you the best face protection. The open-face helmet is good too, but make sure you buy a decent mouth guard. You'll also need a helmet visor to protect and shade your eyes. Try different types until you find the one that suits you best.

Open-faced helmets with mouth guards protect these riders.
Steve Giberson BMX ACTION Magazine

JERSEYS

You can wear pretty much any type jersey for BMX riding or racing. A vented nylon football-type jersey is perfect. Other riders simply wear long-sleeved T-shirts but these don't offer much protection. There are some jerseys you can find which are made of thicker cotton material and come equipped with sewn-in elbow pads.

There are summer jerseys and winter jerseys. The best advice is to shop around and buy both, winter and summer. You'll find in winter, you'll still need an undershirt beneath the jersey to keep warm. You also might want to purchase some elbow guards, especially if you're getting into trick riding.

PANTS

BMX pants are called "leathers," but you won't find much leather in them. They were originally made of leather, but now most pants are made from tough nylon fabrics with stretch panels for more freedom of movement.

They all come with special knee padding and there are differences in how much padding is provided. You have to decide how much padding is comfortable for you when you buy them. Make sure the pants fit. Don't just go by the waist size. They should be comfortable in the thighs and inseams. You need to be able to move around comfortably out there on the track, and you can't concentrate if your pants don't fit right. A good pair of pants with the right amount of knee padding can give you confidence. It's nice to know you'll be protected if you take a spill or two.

GLOVES

Gloves are not required, but it makes sense to wear them while racing. Slide-out and slow speed spills are common, and you can scratch and scrape your hands if you're not wearing gloves. Your hands usually break your fall or cushion your landing, so it's a good idea to own a pair. They also keep you from getting blisters from gripping the handlebars.

You can buy BMX gloves for as low as $10 for the cotton ones and for around $18 and up for the all-leather or the combination leather-and-nylon gloves.

GOGGLES

Why wear goggles? BMX riders don't take chances with their eyes. Besides offering inexpensive protection against eye injury, they also look sharp! A lot of goggles are designed for skiing, so make sure you buy a pair that is specially made for wearing with a helmet. Your BMX dealer will be happy to show you the many varieties offered. There are even mini-goggles to go with the mini BMX helmets.

SOME TIPS

Try on all BMX accessories before you buy. If you're in an area where there are no BMX stores, and you're forced to shop by mail, try on your friends' accessories first. At least you'll get some idea of how they feel. Make sure the company will take it back if it doesn't fit.

MANEUVERS

There's an old story about a guy who had tickets for a rock concert, but he didn't exactly know where the concert hall was. So he stopped someone on the street who happened to be a musician and asked him, "How do you get to the concert hall?" And the musician answered, "Practice, man, practice."

That's what it comes down to in practically anything you do! When you start out on something new, it may look impossible, but step-by-step, little by little, you begin to learn and the next thing you know, you're doing something you were only day-dreaming about a few weeks earlier!

It's easy to become an expert BMX rider. What is an expert on a BMX bike? It's someone who can start, stop, corner and jump. It's simply a matter of practice, man, practice, until you've mastered each and every one of them. The tricks will come later.

So what do you begin with first? Starts? No,

Practice makes perfect as this cyclist proves.
Bob Osborn FREESTYLIN' Magazine

After practicing jumps on small mounds, you'll be ready to get a lot of air!
Steve Giberson BMX ACTION Magazine

you can delay practicing starts until you're ready to go into racing. Stops are easy. All you need are good brakes. What does all this mean? It means that you can begin with the fun part first—jumping!

JUMPS

Assuming you already know how to ride a bike, how many sports let beginners start with the fun part first? Not many, that's for sure! Jumps are what BMX riding is all about, so let's get right to it!

Okay, so you're new, a beginner. You don't know the first thing about taking a jump. It looks pretty scary, doesn't it? Like anything else, it's all in knowing how.

First thing you need is a place to practice. A vacant lot or backyard is perfect. You need a small dirt space where you can build a mound of dirt about five or six inches high, about the size of one of those speed bumps you see in parking lots. Pack it down solid so it won't crumble when you ride over it.

Now that you have your mound of dirt, begin by simply riding slowly over it to get the feel of it. See what it does to you and your bike. After you've done this several times, you have become very familiar with it. Now, speed up a little bit and coast over it. Keep your feet and pedals level (parallel to the ground). Stand, slightly crouched, over the center of your bike. If you're doing this properly, you will be able to ride over the bump without leaving the ground. Your legs and arms will act like shock absorbers and counteract the bump. So you'll simply ride smoothly over it.

To find out what happens if you don't use this proper stance, try coasting over it while sitting on the seat. It'll practically bounce you off the seat! Or try standing up with your legs stiff and straight. You'll be lucky if your feet stay on the pedals!

Now try it again. Stand, slightly crouched, over the center of the bike with your feet and pedals level, and you will roll smoothly over the bump.

Keep doing this until you get it right.

Now speed up a bit. Go fast enough so your wheels will leave the ground a bit. Again, remember, crouch, keep your body over the center of the bike and hold steady. This will keep you from looping over the front end or pitching the rear end up.

Practice this over and over.

The rear wheel lands first in a jump and absorbs the shock of landing.
Windy Osborn BMX ACTION Magazine

HOW TO LAND

When you're coming down from a jump, you want your *rear wheel to land first*. Therefore, you want the front wheel slightly higher than the rear. Ever watch an airplane coming in for a landing? It comes in with the rear angled downward, and the front wheels are the last to touch down. This keeps you in control and makes for a smooth landing. Keep your legs slightly bent at the knees. They will absorb the shock of the rear wheel landing, and the front wheel will touch down smoothly.

How do you get the front wheel up? Simply pull

back slightly on the handlebars as you lift-off from the bump. Don't pull too hard, though. You could flip yourself over! Just a little tug at the right time will get that front wheel up so that you can land on the rear wheel first.

If your front wheel is already coming up, then try leaning a bit more forward toward the front of the bike just as you hit the jump.

Keep practicing this on small jumps until you have gotten it down to perfection. That's an important rule to remember. *Don't go on to the next trick or maneuver until you're absolutely sure you've mastered the first one.*

Want to know a secret? Even the pros don't go over a jump without going over it slowly and checking it out first. Nobody, but nobody goes over a jump without first becoming familiar with it!

CROSS UPS

When you go over a jump and your bike leaves the ground they call it, getting air. That comes from the fact that there is air between you and the ground. Now, once you've begun to get air, you're going to want to learn some tricks or stunts. These are called *cross-ups*. Once again, don't try cross-ups until you are really good at straight jumping!

There are three kinds of cross-ups: Kickouts, Tabletops and One-Footers.

KICKOUTS

To do a kickout, you take a jump, then swivel your hips to make the back wheel go off center to one side or the other. It's kind of a fancy maneuver and adds a little style to your jump.

An enthusiastic crowd cheers this cyclist's tabletop.
Steve Giberson FREESTYLIN' Magazine

TABLETOP

There are varying degrees to this maneuver depending on your ability. It takes a lot of practice, so don't worry if you don't make a complete tabletop right away. Even half a tabletop looks pretty good. What is a tabletop? It is simply a kickout carried one step further. You want to swing your bike out sideways so far that it appears as if the bike is turned flat, or laid-out at the highest part of the jump. The trick is to get back into landing position before you hit the ground. Make sure you're perfect with the kickout before you even begin to try this maneuver.

ONE-FOOTER

In a one-footer, you do a kickout or a tabletop and try and take one foot off the pedal in mid-air and then put it back again before you land.

An awesome one-footer! Bob Osborn FREESTYLIN' Magazine

These are variations on the kickout, and that is what you must master first. Some of you may have seen the movie *The Karate Kid.* It is a lesson in discipline, all about learning the small things first, and soon all the small things add up to a big thing. So if you want to excite your friends with these fancy maneuvers, you must start small.

Start learning your kickout on a small jump. You won't have much time, because you're not in the air that long, but it's enough when you're just beginning.

When you hit the jump and start to *get air,* twist your hips to one side. This will make the rear of the bike swing out. On small jumps you won't be able to swing it out too far, but it's enough so that you'll get the hand of it. Usually, if you do this on small jumps, the rear tire will land off to the side. That's okay. Just remember to keep your front wheel pointed straight in the direction you're headed. This will make it look right.

On bigger jumps, you're going to have harder landings. If you're trying a kickout or a tabletop, you must get the bike back into the upright position before landing. Usually, it's only a matter of reversing your hips to swing it all back into place. If this is difficult for you at this point, then go back and practice straight jumping some more. There's no hurry! You'll get it sooner or later.

CORNERING

Learning how to take corners and berms may not be as flashy as jumping and cross-ups, but this is what helps win races. Corners are where you do a lot of passing in BMX racing.

Some people think going around corners in a great slide means you're a good racer. Nothing could be further from the truth. Good racers know that sliding around corners and turns is a waste of time, and time is one thing racers don't want to waste.

The trick is knowing your bike, your speed and having the feel of just how much traction is left before you begin to slide out.

A good way to learn this is to practice sliding. (Even though, in a race, you don't want to slide). By learning when your bike starts to slide, you'll soon learn how far your bike can go without losing traction.

You practice sliding by doing brake slides. Do this where there's plenty of loose dirt, so you won't

Taking corners right helps win the race. Windy Osborn **BMX ACTION** Magazine

wear out your rear tires so fast.

As you take a turn, hit the brakes. Your rear wheel should skid and start to slide out. Put your inside foot out to act as a brace. Just let it skim along the ground enough to maintain balance. As you do this lean into the slide. Practice this one step until it comes naturally.

Remember, you don't want to slide during a race if you can help it. You're learning slides so you'll be in more control and able to *avoid* slides when possible.

Once you've mastered the brake slide, you are ready to try a corner slide. You simply take the corner fast and lean the bike over so that the tires lose traction and the bike begins to slide. Keep your body weight slightly toward the front of the bike to help the front tires hold traction. Lean into the slide and have your inside foot down to act as a brace as you did in the brake slide.

Practice sliding both to the left and the right. In this manner, you'll soon be able to control your slides.

Once you've learned something, practice it every day. Even the basics you learned when you first started out. Use them as warmups. You never want to lose sight of the basics. Then—try new things!

Always wear your helmet and padding when practicing maneuvers.

1. Back straight. Hips back. Front wheel absolutely straight. Head and shoulders locked, lined up over the headset. Slight bend in the elbows. Take a few deep breaths to relax.

2. Drive your belt buckle into the gooseneck. Keep your head and shoulders back. Drive that pedal as hard as you can.

3. Shift your body back over the bike as quickly as possible to get into your cranking rhythm.

Two-pedal starts are best. BMX ACTION Wizard Publications, Inc.

TIPS ON BMX RACING

Once you've mastered jumping, cornering and a couple of cross-ups, you might want to try BMX racing as a beginner. You also might feel just a little bit nervous about it, because it's an entirely different world, you think. The truth is there's not much difference between BMX racing and the way you normally ride your bike. The difference is—you go faster, and you must learn how to do starts.

BMX racers will tell you that starts are the most important part of a race. It stands to reason if you get off to a good start, you stand a good chance of finishing well in the race. In fact, in most BMX races, the rider who gets off with the best start usually wins! So if you want to win races, practicing starts should be a part of your everyday routine.

Most BMXer's agree, the *two pedal start* is the best. To do this you have to balance against the starting gate with both feet on the pedals. How do you balance without tipping over? Again, practice makes the difference. You can practice balancing against any wall or sidewalk curb. It's going to seem difficult at first. You have to learn how to exert the right amount of pressure so that the front wheel holds steady against the gate.

Remember this. BMX races begin at the top of a hill. The starting gate will angle a bit downhill, so balancing the front wheel against the starting gate is a bit easier. If you can practice against a curb with the same amount of incline, you'll get the feel of it a lot sooner. Don't get upset if you can't master this balancing right away. It can take a few days or even a week to learn how to do it properly.

The next step is learning how to snap out of the starting line when the gate drops down. If you want to pull away ahead of the pack when the gate drops, throw your weight forward the instant it drops. This gives the bike a forward thrust and helps speed up those first few cranks of the wheel. Keep your back straight when you start out and pull up hard on the bars to get more power in your cranks.

TYPES OF GATES

Different tracks have different types of gates. Some have automatic, others have gates that are manually operated. You have to get used to both kinds. Most sanctioned tracks have automatic starting gates with a Christmas tree style light system. This is easier because the timing is consistent. Just stay balanced, watch the lights, get ready and stay relaxed.

Manually operated gates are harder to figure. The gates are operated by hand, and the time after

Jumping too high while racing loses ground.
Steve Giberson BMX ACTION Magazine

the operator shouts, "Get ready!" and the gate drops
can vary. So all you can do is try and keep calm,
listen and not get over anxious and start to soon.

USING JUMPS TO GAIN GROUND

How can you use jumps to gain ground in a race?
The first thing you should learn is that high jumps

(when you take a lot of air) lose ground!

When your bike is in the air, you aren't pedaling. It's as simple as that. If you see racers taking a lot of air on jumps during a race, they are just showing off. There's no time for that in racing.

When you do jumps in a race, you want to keep your bike as *low* as possible to the ground, rather than fly through the air and waste time. BMX races are only a few seconds long and every second counts!

The type of jumping you want to do in a race is called speed-jumping. The nice thing about it is that it's easier to learn than regular jumping. You start out small, just the way you did when learning how to jump.

Practice on a small jump. Just before you hit the jump, do a wheelie. Just pull the front wheel up high enough to clear the top of the jump as you go over it, and then force the front wheel back down again as you go over the jump. As you do this, shift your weight back to keep the rear wheel from kicking up and throwing you over the bars. So, it's pull up the bars just before you go over the jump, then push down on the bars on the other side and at the same time move your weight back to control the rear wheel when you land.

That's how you do it, and it's the same for all types of jumps. On some big jumps it's impossible NOT to take a lot of air! All you can do then is simply try and take the jump as *safely as you can.*

On a big jump, don't try and do a wheelie before you go over. Just take the jump and try and keep your bike as low as possible. You can accomplish this by compressing your body down at the crest of the jump.

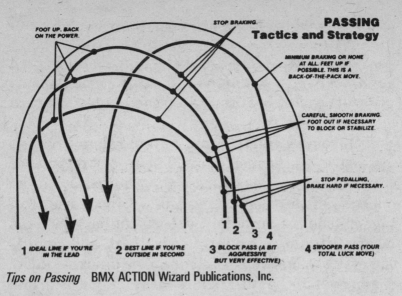

FOOT UP, BACK ON THE POWER.

STOP BRAKING.

MINIMUM BRAKING OR NONE AT ALL. FEET UP IF POSSIBLE. THIS IS A BACK-OF-THE-PACK MOVE.

CAREFUL, SMOOTH BRAKING. FOOT OUT IF NECESSARY TO BLOCK OR STABILIZE.

STOP PEDALLING. BRAKE HARD IF NECESSARY.

1 IDEAL LINE IF YOU'RE IN THE LEAD

2 BEST LINE IF YOU'RE OUTSIDE IN SECOND

3 BLOCK PASS (A BIT AGGRESSIVE BUT VERY EFFECTIVE)

4 SWOOPER PASS (YOUR TOTAL LUCK MOVE)

Tips on Passing   BMX ACTION Wizard Publications, Inc.

PASSING

In racing, passing and protecting (keeping from getting passed) are key factors in winning. You're going to find some racers are stronger pedalers than you. Not to worry. You can beat a stronger rider if you know the right passing maneuvers. Also, there are maneuvers you can learn that will, hopefully, keep racers from passing you.

Most all of BMX passing is set up while taking corners. Again, sliding isn't a good way to take a corner. Try and take corners as smoothly and as quickly as possible without sliding out. Skim your foot along the ground to keep balance when the rear wheel starts to slide.

The best way to learn is to race as much as possible. Don't go out there thinking you're going to win right away. At first, go out there to learn how.

A good passing trick is known as the *block pass*. When the rider you want to pass slows down for a turn, get up enough speed to stay alongside of him and take the inside line. If you are on the inside of the line, it's impossible for the rider next to you to turn comfortably. You are *going in low* on the turn and then *coming out high* on the turn, which means you will be blocking him as you come out of the turn as you go high.

Of course, you're going to find riders who just won't give you the inside line. Then, what do you do?

You try what is called a *slingshot pass*. It's the opposite of the block pass. You approach the turn high and on the outside, and then cut back in. This means you are going into a turn high and coming out of it low. You've got to cut inside quickly and be coming out of the turn before the rider on the inside makes his turn. Timing is everything with the slingshot pass, and you have to watch out or you'll find yourself getting block passed by the entire pack! Just keep in mind that a slingshot pass attempt will leave the inside open. So make certain that no other riders are close enough inside to take advantage of you.

If you're going to become a BMX racer, you must practice every day. And the most important part of your practice should be the starts.

Always warm up before a race by riding your bike at least fifteen minutes beforehand. Don't take jumps that you are unsure of. Your safety comes first. Work up to the big jumps. They take a lot of practice.

Remember, you should make yourself familiar with the jumps and the track before the race, if at all possible.

COMPETITION INFORMATION

Riders are classified by age and ability. If you are thirteen years old and racing for the first time, you would be put in the thirteen beginner group, and so on.

First you sign up for the races. Then all the racers' names and their classifications are arranged into heats called *motos*. The moto sheets are posted so you can see what race you will be in. There are eight riders in each moto. Each set of motos is called to the starting line to race three times. After the third moto, all the results are added up and the best riders are awarded their prizes. If there is further competition that day, new sheets are posted listing the riders who qualify.

Riders are divided equally into separate motos. At the end of the third set of motos, the top qualifying riders from each moto set meet in the main event.

Concentration is an important part of BMXing.
BMX ACTION Magazine Wizard Publications, Inc.

If there are a lot of riders, they are divided equally into as many motos as it takes to have a maximum of eight riders each. At the end of the first three sets of motos, the top qualifying riders are transferred into *Semi-mains,* which are one-race elimination heats. The semi-mains determine which riders will compete in the main event. Semi-mains don't always happen. It depends on how many riders are there that day to compete.

After three motos for each group, everyone has had a chance to qualify. There are two methods for deciding who qualifies for the semi-main or the main. One is the *low-points* system and the other is the *transfer* system.

The low points system is the Olympic scoring method. For example, if you come in first, you score one point. If you come in second, you score two points, and so on. After the three initial motos, your points are added up. The ones with the lowest score have qualified for the main event. (Or the semi-

Ride, racer, ride! Steve Giberson BMX ACTION Magazine

mains if there are a lot of riders that day.) The lowest scores in the semi-mains will then go on to the main event.

All BMX associations use the low-points system except the ABA. The ABA prefers the transfer system, because they don't count anyone except those riders who came in first in each moto.

It works like this. If a rider finishes first in one of the three initial motos, he or she is automatically *transferred* to the semi-main or the main. So that rider doesn't get to race again until the semi-main or main.

A lot of riders object to this transfer method, because it means if they should win the first moto, they'd have to wait around all day until the semi-main or main event comes up before they can race again.

As you can see, BMX scoring systems are very simple. It's just a matter of which system is used by the track that holds the competition.

In progress. Bob Osborn FREESTYLIN' Magazine

BUILDING YOUR OWN BACKYARD BMX TRACK

It's easy to build a good BMX track. All you need is a vacant lot and the owner's permission. Tracks aren't made out of anything, either. They are just dirt. The problem is moving the dirt around and building it up.

The first thing you have to do is design the track. Take a good look at the land and amount of space you have to work with. Draw the track design on a piece of paper. Work out exactly where you want the jumps and turns. Remember, you must keep the design safe enough for the young riders and interesting enough for the more experienced ones. Safety comes first, always. A badly designed turn, for example, could cause accidents.

For your first track, it is best to make the jumps fairly easy. You can always build them up later when the riders become more expert. Again, it's simply a matter of pushing the dirt around.

If you know someone who owns a tractor, you're really in luck. A tractor can save a lot of time and energy. They can be rented, by the way, if you have someone with a license to drive and knows how to operate one.

Try to build up a good starting hill. This backyard lot is going to be just for practice, but a good starting hill or incline will give you the feel of a real track.

Once you've dug out the track in the design you've created, use the excess dirt to build up your jumps. Pack it down and repack it until they are firm. You don't want your jumps to crumble after repeated use.

Most of the turns should have a berm on the outside. Wide turns should be banked like a *Daytona turn*. That's a high-banked turn like those Daytona Raceway turns in Florida. The steepest part of the bank should be the last half of the turn, because that's the part of the turn where the riders tend to go upwards toward the outside.

You can make your jumps as big as you want, but always keep in mind the safety factor. You can put jumps anywhere you think they would be fun. You can even throw one in at the end of a turn!

Some *whoop-de-doos* are always fun to add to any track. Whoop-de-doos are just rounded mounds of dirt that stretch across the track (like those speed bumps you see in parking lots at malls). Usually, they are placed three in a row. These whoops can be anywhere from three to twelve inches high. Any larger than that and they will become jumps. Whoop-de-doos are fun and really add a lot of excitement to any track.

Finished at last and ready for the riders. Bob Osborn FREESTYLIN' Magazine

Jumps are the most exciting part of any BMX race. Build them so the expert riders can *take air*, but still are safe for the mini-riders. Make sure the jumps are ramped on both sides and are rounded at the top, so you can ride smoothly over them if you choose not to jump. Don't ever build a jump that drops off at the edge. Make sure it slopes down smoothly. Remember, radical jumps that drop-off are for Pro riders only!

Make it a rule at your track that anyone riding there must wear and use proper safety gear. If you start holding organized races at your track, you will have to get insurance. Talk to your parents or other BMX experts about that.

A place to practice is any BMXer's dream.
Steve Giberson BMX ACTION Magazine

ORGANIZED RACES

Perhaps, you want to get an official BMX track started in your community. If so, then you will need some backing. Contact local groups and organizations like YMCAs, Police Athletic Leagues, Boys Clubs of America, lodges like the Elks or clubs such as the Lions or Rotary. These groups are always looking for something to do for young people, and BMX racing has such a good reputation as a sport and its safety record is so perfect, that you'll have no trouble getting some group interested. Sometimes even a group of parents have joined together to form a BMX club. A good place to start talking this up is at your local BMX bike dealer.

These groups can help find the land to build your official track on. It's a good idea to have the track close enough into town so people can ride their

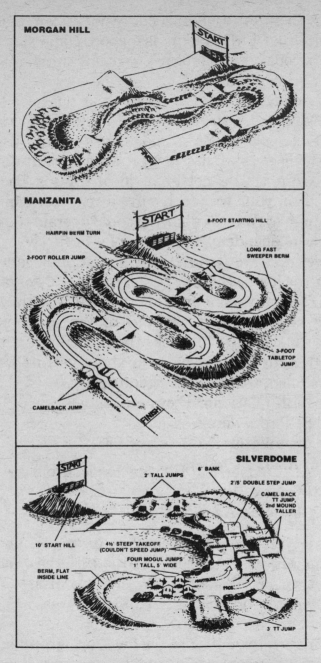

MORGAN HILL

START

MANZANITA

START

HAIRPIN BERM TURN

8-FOOT STARTING HILL

2-FOOT ROLLER JUMP

LONG FAST
SWEEPER BERM

3-FOOT
TABLETOP
JUMP

CAMELBACK JUMP

FINISH

SILVERDOME

START

2' TALL JUMPS

6' BANK

2'/5' DOUBLE STEP JUMP

CAMEL BACK
TT JUMP;
2nd MOUND
TALLER

10' START HILL

4½' STEEP TAKEOFF
(COULDN'T SPEED JUMP)

FOUR MOGUL JUMPS
1' TALL, 5' WIDE

BERM, FLAT
INSIDE LINE

3' TT JUMP

Different tracks offer different BMXing delights, from hills to hairpins to double jumps to Camelbacks! BMX ACTION Wizard Publications, Inc.

bikes there. As soon as local residents are made to realize that BMX racing is a good, clean sport just like baseball, you shouldn't have any trouble getting their cooperation.

Remember, a lot of people may not have heard of BMX racing, so you'll have to explain it to them. Take along some BMX magazines so they can see for themselves what a fast-growing sport it is.

Once you've gotten a local group's backing, you're on your way to having a real track in your community. Your local group could operate the track as an independent and have a lot of fun with that. However, if you want official national sanction, your track must be a part of a nationwide organization. The two major ones are the NBL and the ABA. They have special plans, rules and regulations that are available only to tracks they officially sanction.

For further information about getting a track sanctioned, write to these addresses:

NBL (National Bicycle League)
84 Park Avenue
Flemington, New Jersey 08822

ABA (American Bicycle Association)
P.O. Box 718
Chandler, AZ. 85224

Which one you choose is up to you and the group. The best guideline is to go with the organization that has the most members in your area. That way you can organize more official races.

Remember, proper instruction, training and safety equipment are a must before anyone participates in this sport.

SOME BMX STARS

The top US professional riders are Greg Hill and Stu Thomsen. Currently, they are BMX's all-time top money earners.

Greg went pro at age fourteen, and has been a top money earner three times. He also won the first three Pro World Championships and came in second the fourth time around.

Stu, twenty-seven, is the oldest of the original pros. He plans to keep racing until he stops winning. Stu is now with Huffy.

Others who have gained fame are:

TIM MARCH—One of Britain's top riders, Tim has won the United Kingdom Number 1 plates two times and has taken two European titles. He also designs and makes number plates.

HARRY LEARY—One of the first pros in BMX racing, Harry rides for Diamond Back and six co-sponsors. Known for his aggressive riding, he is called

Riding high! Bob Osborn FREESTYLIN' Magazine

Scary Leary.

ALICE TEMPLE—Alice was the first girl to win the girl's Number 1 plate two years in a row.

JASON JENSEN—He's won more than 2,000 trophies and does commercials for Wheaties and Kool-aid.

CLINT MILLER—A pro racer since the early days, his biggest win so far was the IBMXF International in Holland.

BRENT PATTERSON—Brent is twenty-four and rides pro for his own company, Patterson Racing Products. He was top ABA in 1980 and comes from northern California.

BRIAN PATTERSON—Brian is Brent Patterson's younger brother. In 1983, Brian won more races than any other pro, but he lost the NBL Number 1 Pro Plate to Eric Rupe.

ERIC AND ROBBY RUPE—Eric, twenty-one and Robby, twenty-three, are the other top BMX racing brothers. Eric won the 1983 NBL Number 1 Pro Plate. They are from southern California.

ANTHONY SEWELL—He won both the NBL and the ABA Number 1 pro plates in 1980. He is on the Murray Team.

TOBY HENDERSON—Toby won the 1983 Grand National. His sponsor is Hutch Performance Products.

MIKE MIRANDA—Mike won the very first pro race he entered, the 1982 Mongoose International at Magic Mountain. He is from Southern California and rides for the ICW team.

"LITTLE" EDDY KING—When Eddy became a pro in 1983, he lead most of the ESPN TV racing series. He rides for the Diamond Back Racing Team.

GARY ELLIS—Gary has earned a Number 1 ranking by the ABA in his class. He is from Washington and rides for Kuwahara.

TOMMY BRACKENS—In 1982, Tommy won several NBL Nationals. He rides for Team Powerlite.

Photos by Bob Osborn FREESTYLIN' Magazine

Steve Giberson BMX ACTION Magazine

Fancy Freestylin' Maneuvers

GLOSSARY OF TERMS

BMX: Bicycle motocross

BERM: A banked bend in a racing track. The term originally came from motorbike motocross racing. Every BMX track has at least three.

CRANKING: Pedaling very hard.

FREESTYLING: Trick or stunt riding.

GETTING AIR: When your bike flies through the air. The space (air) between your bike and the ground.

GNARLY: Difficult, hard to do.

THE HOLESHOT: There are different meanings to this. It all depends on where you're from. To some it means the rider who gets out of the gate first. To others it means the rider who gets to the first obstacle first. Still others believe it's the rider who gets to the first turn first. Take your pick.

MOTO: A race, or heat.

RAD: Simply an abbreviation of the word "radical." Used to describe something crazy or off-the-wall.

SPEEDJUMPING: Going over a jump without taking too much air. The idea is to keep your wheels as close to the ground as possible and keep pedaling all through the jump. Wheelie before the jump, keep pedaling and shift weight to the rear wheel.

THE TABLETOP: A great freestyler's trick. It's called a tabletop because as you take air from a jump, you lay your bike out flat like a table. How well you do it depends on the degree of flatness you achieve. Perfect is plain flat. You must be good to do this, because you have to go "flat" and then flip back and land upright all in the space of a few seconds. Before you can even attempt this, you must learn bunny hopping.

THE BUNNY HOP: A maneuver, once mastered, that enables you to jump clear over rocks, ditches, tree stumps or any other obstacle that comes across your path.

WHEELIE: The art of traveling on one wheel. This is accomplished by lifting up the front wheel and riding along on the rear wheel. Used in BMX racing to set up speedjumps.

WHOOP-DE-DOO: Closely spaced mounds in a BMX track.

WIRED: In control. Knowing a trick well enough to do it right, again and again.